The African Slave Trade

The African Slave Trade

Shirlee P. Newman

Watts LIBRARY

Franklin Watts
A Division of Grolier Publishing
New York • London • Hong Kong • Sydney
Danbury, Connecticut

For Haley, Julie, Laura, Abby, and David

Note to readers: Definitions for words in **bold** can be found in the Glossary at the back of this book.

Photographs ©: AKG London: 43; Archive Photos: 8, 12, 52; Art Resource, NY: 13 (Erich Lessing); Bridgeman Art Library International Ltd., London/New York: 6 (EX17082/Portrait of a Negro Man, Olaudah Equiano, 1780's, (previously attributed to Joshua Reynolds). 18th Century. Oil on canvas, 61.8 x 51.5 cm. Royal Albert Memorial Museum, Exeter, Devon, UK), 33 (BAL126339/Hoeing Rice, illustration from 'Harper's Weekly', 1867, from 'The Pageant of America, Vol. 3', by Ralph Henry Gabriel, by Alfred R. Waud. 1926. Engraving. Private Collection), 40 (WHM112027/Wedgewood jasper medallion decorated with a slave in chains and inscribed with 'Am I not a Man and a Brother',1790's. Ceramic./Wilberforce House, Hull City Museums and Art Galleries, UK), 44 (MGS118663/'Tippo-Tip', Zanzibar, c. 1890, by E. C. Dias. Photographed with gelatin printing-out paper, 20 x 15.2 cm. Private Collection/Michael Graham-Stewart), 50 (STC93653/Boors Returning from Hunting, plate 11 from 'African Scenery and Animals', by Samuel Daniell. Engraved by the artist. Coloured aquatint. 1804. Private Collection/The Stapleton Collection), 48, 49 (BON101602/The East Indiaman 't Slot ter Hooge' and other shipping in a brisk breeze off a Dutch port, possibly Flushing, by Engel Hoogerheyden. 18th Century. Oil on canvas, 86.4 x 137 cm. Private Collection/Bonhams, London, UK); Corbis-Bettmann: 35 (Macmillan/McGraw-Hill), 2, 19, 22, 28, 31, 46; Mary Evans Picture Library: 11, 14, 15, 18, 38, 41; New Haven Colony Historical Society: 24, 25; North Wind Picture Archives: 5, 16, 26, 36, 42; Superstock, Inc.: 45; The Art Archive: 20.

Cover illustration by Carol Werner.

Visit Franklin Watts on the Internet at:
http://publishing.grolier.com

Library of Congress Cataloging-in-Publication Data

Newman, Shirlee Petkin.
    The African slave trade / by Shirlee P. Newman
        p.   cm.— (Watts Library)
    Includes bibliographical references and index.
    ISBN 0-531-11694-8 (lib. bdg.)   0-531-16537-X (pbk.)
    1. Slave trade—Africa—History—Juvenile literature. 2. Slave trade—United States—History—Juvenile literature. 3. Slaves—United States—Social conditions—Juvenile literature. [1. Slave trade. 2. Slaves.] I. Title. II. Series.
HT1322 .N38 2000
380.1'44'096—dc21
                                                  00-038198

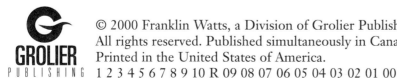

Contents

Olaudah Equiano, shown in this 1780s portrait, wrote about his experiences as a slave stolen from Africa.

Chapter One

Slavery in Africa

"One day when all our people had gone . . . and only I and my dear sister were left to mind the house, two men and a woman got over our walls and seized us both," Olaudah Equiano wrote, years later in a book about his life. Olaudah was eleven when he and his sister were kidnapped in 1760 in what is today Gambia. His captors separated them. One of the men stuffed Olaudah into a bag and tossed him over his shoulder like a sack of grain. Olaudah was sold and resold as

Arab slave traders take captured blacks to be sold as slaves.

a slave. He escaped, returned home, and was kidnapped again. This time his kidnappers took him downriver to the sea and sold him to an English sea captain.

Europeans had been kidnapping and selling African men, women, and children long before Olaudah Equiano was kidnapped. Before the Europeans arrived in the 1400s, Africans had been in the business of slave trading for hundreds of years. As early as 300 B.C., North African Arabs sold black Africans to slave markets in the Middle East.

Arab slave traders in northeast Africa took slaves across the Sahara Desert and sold them in the northwest. Many died on the journey of heat stroke, exhaustion, or thirst. Some of those who survived were shipped across the Mediterranean Sea and sold in Europe. Arab slave traders also sold people from the West Coast and East Africa. Along with Arab traders, African groups raided neighboring groups' village just to get slaves.

Many people today might wonder why Africans traded other Africans. Africa is a huge continent, made up of hundreds of different groups, or tribes. The people identified with members of their own group. Just as the French and the Dutch are different nationalities, so too are the Yoruba people and the Hausa people, for example. When the Yoruba defeated the Hausa, they sold the Hausa they captured into slavery.

A Slave's Life in Africa

Most slaves sold within Africa were prisoners of war. Some slaves, like Olaudah Equiano, were kidnapped and sold into slavery by slave traders (also called slavers) while others were enslaved as punishment for crimes they committed. When food was scarce, African parents often sold their children so that they would be fed. Some people enslaved themselves to pay back debts. Also, in some areas, people who kidnapped people and sold them into slavery could themselves be enslaved. A baby born to a slave mother belonged to the mother's owner.

Slaves in Africa were not treated as brutally as slaves in other countries. Household slaves were often considered part of the family. "After many days of traveling, I got into the

From Royalty to Slavery

Even chiefs or other members of African royalty could become slaves. Ibrahama, a prince of the Fulbe people, studied geography, astronomy, mathematics, religion, and law at schools in the African cities of Jenne and Timbuktu. At age seventeen, Ibrahama joined the army and later became a prisoner of war. He was sold to an English sea captain, taken to America, and sold into slavery in Mississippi.

Prince Ukasaw, the son of a Nigerian king, was also enslaved. An Arab merchant invited the prince to come with him to see "a house with wings that walks on water." The "winged house" was a Dutch slave ship. The Arab merchant sold the prince to the Dutch sea captain.

hands of a chieftain," Olaudah Equiano wrote. "This man had two wives and some children, and they all treated me extremely well." In tribes such as the Ashanti of the Gold Coast (now Ghana), a slave could marry, own property, and even inherit some of his master's property. Some slaves had slaves of their own, and a few became kings after the ruler who had owned them died.

Some slaves served as soldiers, and some rose through the ranks to positions of authority. Others mined gold and salt, or collected ivory elephant tusks and rubber from trees. Slaves also worked on large farms called **plantations**.

African Slavers Raid Villages

To capture their victims, African slave raiders on horseback often surrounded African villages. They burned down the houses and chased anyone who tried to escape. The raiders chained or tied the captives together in **coffles**, or lines, and attached them to the horses' tails. Raids on farmers in fields had to be carried out quickly so the raiders could escape if anyone tried to attack them. The raiders kept the slaves chained together in outdoor pens called **barracoons** or in earthen pits. Before the Europeans came to Africa, the slave raiders would trade slaves with other African groups.

African slavers attack a village to get slaves.

Muslim slavers transport captives to the coastal ports in Africa.

After the Europeans arrived, the demand for slaves increased. Europeans often traded goods for slaves with African slave raiders or traders. Sometimes Europeans would conduct slave raids of their own or hire African slave raiders to do the work for them.

The Europeans built about forty castles or forts on the coast as storage places for the people they bought or kidnapped. The Portuguese built Elmina Fort on a high cliff overlooking the Atlantic Ocean in what is now Ghana. Elmina could hold one thousand slaves at a time. It had high towers and walls that were 30 feet (10 meters) thick. It was surrounded by two

The Door of No Return

On Gorée Island, 2 miles (3 kilometers) off the coast of what is now Senegal, traders kept slaves in dark cellars under their homes until the slaves boarded a ship. Today, visitors to Gorée Island can stand in the doorway that led out to slaver ships and try to imagine how Africans felt as they left to become slaves in an unknown country.

moats—trenches filled with water—and defended by four hundred cannons. Slaves from central Africa were chained together and marched for hundreds of miles or paddled down long, winding rivers to such storage places on the coast to await a slave ship. Over the years, the European forts kept changing hands because traders from the different countries competed for slaves. England, France, and Holland finally became the most active ones in the slave-trading industry.

Africans Cooperate with Europeans

Rulers Against Slave Trade

Although some African rulers engaged in the slave trade, other African rulers fought against it. Queen Nzinga who ruled the land that is now Angola protected escaped slaves. In the 1600s, she led her army in small-scale attacks against Portuguese slave traders.

Many African communities were just as eager to make money on the slave trade as European countries were. Over the years, several African rulers sold slaves to European traders. In 1726, King Agaja of Dahomey (now Benin) sent forty slaves to King George I of England with a letter. King Agaja wanted to buy "quality goods," he said in the letter. He even mentioned that he would trade ". . . a thousand slaves for any single thing." By "quality goods," King Agaja meant guns and gunpowder, fabrics, iron bars, tobacco, liquor, gold, and **cowrie shells**, which some African tribes used as money.

"Guns and gunpowder have been the most popular merchandise here for a long time," a Dutch slave trader wrote in his diary. "If we did not supply them, we would not get our share of the [slave] trade."

A European slave trader in Africa exchanges goods for people.

Slaves crowded together on the deck of the slave ship Wildfire.

Chapter Two

The Journey

Starting from one of the trading ports on Africa's West Coast, slaves faced a long, difficult voyage. At first, the Europeans took the slaves to Europe and sold them there. Later, when the colonists from various European countries had settled in the Americas, slaves were usually taken across the Atlantic Ocean and traded for molasses, sugar, and rum. Then these were taken back to Europe and traded for morc goods to trade for more slaves. The trip from West Africa to America was called the "Middle Passage," and took about forty-five days. Later, some slave

ships sailed down Africa's West Coast, around the Cape of Good Hope, and up the East Coast to kidnap or trade for slaves. The trip from the East Coast to America took two or three months.

The ships' crew treated the slaves like **cargo** or animals. "When I was carried aboard, I was handled and tossed up to see if I were [healthy] by some of the crew," Olaudah Equiano wrote. He had never seen white people before, and someone had told him that whites ate blacks. He fainted when he saw a big pot of water boiling over a fire because he thought that the slavers planned to cook him in it. Slaves in Africa were never treated nearly as cruelly as they were treated on that ship, he

*A trader brands a
healthy slave before
the trip overseas.*

wrote later. He would gladly have changed places with any
slave in his own country.

Most slaves were examined before they were taken on board
the ship that would take them to the Americas. Their muscles
and joints were pinched; their teeth, eyes, and chests were
poked. Healthy slaves were branded with the initials of the

Slaves on the **Albanez** *were often hungry and were crowded on top of one another.*

Illness At Sea

One **helmsman** (the person who steers a ship) and most of the crew and slaves on a French ship called the *Rodeur* caught a disease called **ophthalmia**—an inflammation, or swelling, of the eye that caused temporary or sometimes permanent blindness. After surviving a storm, the *Rodeur* lost its way and called out to a Spanish vessel for help. Help never came. Everyone on the Spanish ship was blind too. Finally, the *Rodeur's* helmsman's eyes cleared up, and the ship docked at Guadeloupe, a French island in the West Indies. The captain had thrown thirty-nine blind slaves overboard. The Spanish ship never reached port. No one knows what became of it.

person or company to whom they now belonged. Branding was done with a red-hot iron on the chest, shoulder, or cheek.

During the day, the women and children were sometimes allowed up on deck. At night, all slaves were kept below deck in the **hold**—the space used to store cargo. It was so crowded that each person scarcely had enough room to turn. To prevent slaves from jumping overboard, they were chained together at their ankles and wrists until the African shore was out of sight.

The captains of most slave ships thought they could make more money by carrying as many slaves as they could pack in, even if more of them died because of overcrowding. Slaves on some ships had to lie on rough, wooden shelves built so close together that the people couldn't sit up. On other ships, space was so scarce that they couldn't lie down at all.

Thousands of slaves died or killed themselves on the trips to the Americas. For example, one Portuguese ship left Africa with 1,200 slaves and arrived in Brazil, South America, with

Food and Water on Board

In the 1600s, slaves on ships were fed mainly on grain mixed with water, which was cooked until it was thick. Fruit, biscuits, beans, and a bit of salted beef were added in the 1700s. When slaves tried to starve themselves to death, their mouths were forced open with metal instruments and food was stuffed inside.

Toward the end of the journey, they were usually given more food to fatten them up for sale. Some slaves were taken to a farm after they landed and fattened up before they were sold.

Water for slaves was limited. Sometimes they were given only one cup of water a day. On many ships, the water was stored in unclean barrels, causing sickness or death.

only 600. Schools of sharks often followed the ships, waiting for bodies tossed overboard (or slaves who jumped).

Children often fell into the big open tubs used as toilets. It was so hot in the hold and the air smelled so terrible that some slaves suffocated. On some ships, two or three slaves were found dead each morning.

When seas were calm, slaves were sometimes taken up on deck for a while. With a whip cracking over their heads, they were forced to sing and dance to get some exercise and amuse the crew. During stormy weather, the slaves were kept in the hold. Seasickness, caused by the rolling sea, made people to vomit, which made the smell of the hold even worse.

Slaves Revolt

Most slave revolts, or rebellions, took place either before or shortly after ships set sail from Africa. They usually failed because unarmed slaves were no match for sailors with guns and cutlasses. The crew of the ship had many ways to punish the rebel slaves—the sailors whipped, choked, strangled,

Tomba, a Brave Leader

Some English traders enslaved Tomba, an African leader in what is now Guinea, because he tried to convince other African leaders to resist the slave trade. Tomba was in the hold of the ship called the *Robert* when a female slave brought him a hammer. Tomba, one other slave, and the enslaved woman crept up on deck where some sailors were sleeping. Just as Tomba struck a sleeping sailor on the head, Captain Harding and the rest of the crew appeared on deck.

Tomba and the other slaves were shackled, or locked, into heavy iron rings. The men were whipped severely, but were allowed to live because they were strong and would bring a good price. The female slave was hoisted up by her thumbs, whipped, and stabbed to death.

hung, shot, dismembered (cut off parts of the body), or drowned those involved in revolts.

In 1532, a hundred slaves on a Portuguese ship called the *Misericordia* broke loose from their chains and killed all but three of the crew. The three surviving sailors escaped in a

longboat (the largest boat carried on a merchant sailing vessel), but no one knows what happened to the slaves. Thirty years later a Spanish ship was wrecked off the coast of South America, and the captive slaves killed the sailors who survived the wreck. A slave named Illescas remained in South America and became a leader of Indians there.

In the 1700s, an English sea captain anchored his ship in a river in Africa. He invited several Africans to come aboard to trade, but instead, the ship sailed away with them. It reached the ocean but was driven back to the river, perhaps by a storm, and forced to anchor in the spot where the kidnapping had taken place. Some Africans who lived near the river boarded the ship, killed most of the crew, and freed the captives.

In the 1730s, ninety-six Africans on the English ship *Little George* managed to take control of the ship and tossed some of the crew overboard. The other sailors and the captain, armed with guns, locked themselves in a cabin, expecting the Africans to surrender because they couldn't steer the ship. They were mistaken. The Africans sailed the ship back to Africa and escaped.

When the Journey Ended

When slave ships arrived in the Americas, the slaves who survived the trip were sometimes sold in a scramble, a kind of free-for-all sale. Buyers all dashed into the slave pen at once and grabbed the slaves they wanted. Ouladah Equiano was sold in a scramble when he landed in Barbados, a British island in the West Indies. "Relations and friends were separated," he wrote. Most of them never saw each other again.

Slaves who were not sold were called **refuse**, or trash, and offered at reduced prices. Those who were still not sold were

Slavers advertised their slave sales in the local newspapers, as shown above in this ad from the Charles Town Gazette *in 1744.*

TO BE SOLD *by* William Yeomans, (*in Charles Town Merchant,*) a parcel of good Plantation Slaves. Encouragement will be given by taking Rice in Payment, or any Time Credit, Security to be given if required There's likewise to be sold, very good Troopleg saddles and Furniture, choice Barbados and Boston Rum, also Cordial Waters and Limejuice, as well as a parcel of extraordinary Indian trading Goods, and many of other sorts suitable for the Season.

often left on the docks without food or water. Slaves on the islands rescued some of them, but many died of starvation or thirst.

When slaves reached Charles Town, South Carolina, they spent ten days in the **pest house** to make sure that none of the slaves had any diseases. The pest house was located on an island in the harbor and used as a place to keep diseased people. If anyone on the ship had smallpox, for example, the slaves stayed in the pest house for a month. A landing, or dock, near Charles Town is still called Igbo Landing, because so many Igbo people from West Africa tried to commit suicide by jumping into the water there.

Charles Town's Name Change

Charles Town, South Carolina, was named for King Charles II of England. Its name was changed to Charleston in 1783, after the Revolutionary War.

Slaves arrive at the Jamestown Colony in Virginia.

Chapter Three

Trading Slaves in America

In 1619, the year before the *Mayflower* landed in what is now Massachusetts, twenty Africans were brought to the English colony of Jamestown, Virginia, on a Dutch ship. The ship's captain sold some of the Africans to the colonists as **indentured servants**—people who had to work without pay for several years. Some were freed after they had worked the required length of time; others were held as slaves for life.

By the end of the century, large plantations were being developed in the southern American colonies. Soon, every African brought to the New World, or born into slavery, was considered a slave.

By the middle 1700s, slave merchants and **agents** were common in coastal cities from Maine to Georgia. The most active slave ports were smaller cities such as Newport and Bristol, Rhode Island, and Charleston, South Carolina. Merchants, ship owners, agents and captains dealing in slaves also worked in larger cities such as Philadelphia, Pennsylvania, New York, New York, and Boston, Massachusetts.

Boston and other New England cities were also centers for shipbuilding. Ships built in the colonies were usually much smaller than those built in England, and were run by a smaller crew. The *Desire*, the first ship from America to carry slaves, was built in Marblehead, Massachusetts. The *Desire* sailed from nearby Salem in 1638 with a cargo of Pequots—American Indians taken by the English as prisoners of war. After selling the Pequots in the British West Indies, William Pierce, the *Desire*'s captain, returned to New England with cotton, tobacco, salt, and some black slaves, whom he sold in Connecticut.

Fifteen years after the *Desire*'s first trip, some businessmen in Boston

Tobacco for Virginia

John Rolfe, an early settler in Jamestown married Pocahontas, the daughter of an American Indian chief. John Rolfe brought tobacco seeds from the West Indies and grew them in Virginia. In 1614, he shipped the dried tobacco leaves to Europe and the product became popular. Only a few years later, planters in Virginia sent 50,000 pounds (22,680 kilograms) of tobacco to Europe. Planters made a lot of money from tobacco, making the crop very important to the economy of the colony.

A slave trader holds a public auction outside.

supplied money to build three larger ships, hire crews, and buy provisions. One of the ships, the *Rainbow*, sailed to Africa in search of gold, silver, ivory, and slaves. On the way back, the *Rainbow* stopped in the West Indies, and traded the slaves for wine, sugar, salt, and tobacco to sell in New England.

The Gift Called Rice

A legend some historians believe to be true says that in the late 1600s a ship from Madagascar, an island off the west of Africa, took refuge from a storm in Charles Town's harbor. The ship's captain gave Carolina's governor some seeds—the origin of the colony's profitable rice crops.

Carolina's low coastal plain, divided from the ocean by marshes was ideal for growing rice. Because rice could not grow in England's cold climate, Carolina's planters had no idea how to grow rice. But the slaves knew how. Slaves who came from Africa's rice-growing regions built dams to keep salt water from flowing into the marshes where rice was planted. They cleared the trees and undergrowth from the area and dug the canals and ditches for the rice fields. The slaves planted and tended to the rice crops. At harvest time, the slaves cut down the stalks of the rice plants and threshed (beat the grains from the husks) them, and loaded the rice onto

From Rags to Riches

Georgia was founded as a colony for poor English people in 1733. At first, Georgia's colonial officials would not allow slavery because they thought slave labor would promote laziness among the poor. The rule against slavery was changed in 1749 because slave owners in Carolina, just to the north, were getting rich. After slave labor was allowed, rice and cotton plantations were developed in Georgia, and some Georgia planters also became rich.

Slaves show southern plantation owners (or planters) how to cultivate rice.

barges. Then the slaves took the rice down Carolina's rivers to the ocean where it shipped to England and sold for high prices.

A New Country Is Born

The first meeting of the Continental Congress was held in Philadelphia, Pennsylvania, in October 1774. The delegates met to discuss problems the colonies had with Great Britain, but they also passed a resolution stating they would not allow any more slaves into the colonies. The British government refused to follow the resolution because many prominent Englishmen had invested a great deal of money in the Royal Africa Company, which supplied most of the colonies' slaves.

When the colonies decided to free themselves from Britain, Thomas Jefferson, a Virginia lawyer who attended the Continental Congress, wrote the Declaration of Independence stating why the colonists wanted to be free. He mentioned slavery in the first draft, but the Carolina colony insisted that the mention of slavery be removed.

During the Revolutionary War (1775–1783), the slave business declined. Some slave ships became pirate ships or privateers—privately owned vessels that were allowed to capture enemy ships. The captain of one English privateer gave fifty Africans on his ship guns to help fight a French ship off the coast of the West Indies. The slaves fought well, the captain noted in his daily logbook as he sailed to the island of Jamaica to sell them.

However, an increased interest in growing cotton spurred new interest in slavery after the war. By the 1790s, planters in some southern states had worn out the soil for their crops. At the time, Europe had become **glutted**, or overloaded, with tobacco because it was also grown in Spain, the Spanish West Indies, and the Dutch East Indies (now Indonesia). Other crops, such as rice and **indigo** (a plant used to dye fabric blue), were no longer as profitable as they once had been. However, new machinery developed in England had increased the demand for raw cotton. Eli Whitney, a New England school teacher, had invented the cotton gin—an engine that separated cotton fiber from seeds much faster than it could be done

Slaves operate the cotton gin while their owners inspect the cotton.

Important Citizens Deal in Slaves

Slavery was a way of life in colonial America, as it had been in other places since prehistoric times. Many men who were respected in their community were active in the slave trade. For example, Peter Faneuil, who built Boston's Faneuil Hall, was part owner of a slave ship. Philadelphia's Robert Morris, called the Revolutionary War's financier because he raised so much money for the army, was also a slave trader. John Paul Jones, known as the father of the American Navy because of his heroism in the war, had been a crewman on slave ships. George Washington, Thomas Jefferson, James Monroe, James Madison, Andrew Jackson, and several other presidents of the United States were slave owners.

by hand. Soon, cotton was a major crop, with some plantations covering 2,000 to 3,000 acres (810 to 1,200 hectares). As a result, American planters wanted even more slave laborers.

Thomas Clarkson was a leading abolitionist in England.

Chapter Four

Banning Slave Trade

In 1785, Thomas Clarkson, an English college student, read about the evils of slavery and wrote a prize-winning essay entitled "Is it Lawful to Make Slaves of Others Against Their Will?" Clarkson also decided to do whatever he could to abolish the slave trade. He went to Liverpool and other English slave ports, and spoke with sailors on the docks. He visited taverns where young men were encouraged to drink too much liquor and were then taken onto slave ships and

Poems and Songs Against Slavery

American and British poets wrote poems against the slave trade. Musicians put the words to music, and the songs were sung at meetings of antislavery societies in England and the United States. Josiah Wedgwood, a famous English potter, created a **cameo**—a small sculpture—as the symbol of the antislavery movement. The cameo showed a kneeling black man with his arms and legs in chains saying: "Am I not a man and a brother?" The cameos adorned snuffboxes, and were worn as brooches, bracelets, and hatpins on both sides of the Atlantic.

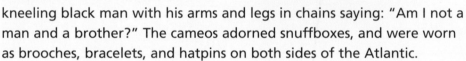

forced to serve as crewmen. Clarkson also inspected slave ships and spoke to ships' doctors, retired slave traders, and sea captains. He collected cruel instruments such as shackles, chains, thumbscrews, and metal mouth openers. He spent hours in **customs houses**, buildings in which shipping records were kept, taking notes on ships' arrivals, departures, and cargoes.

While seeking information about the treatment of slaves, Clarkson also found records about the British seamen who worked on slave ships. He learned that less than half of the British seamen who sailed to Africa ever came back, and most who did were sick for the rest of their lives. One day, Clarkson spoke with a sailor who had recently seen the captain of his ship murder another seaman. As Clarkson was leaving the dock, a gang of rough-looking men tried to attack him. Clarkson escaped and continued to investigate the slave trade despite the attack. He wrote and spoke against the slave trade for the rest of his life.

In 1789, William Wilberforce presented the evidence that Clarkson had collected to Parliament, Britain's lawmaking body, but a law to ban the slave trade was voted down. English manufacturers, shipbuilders, and slave traders were afraid they would lose money. However, in 1807, Parliament passed a law banning the slave trade, and the United States banned the importation of slaves in 1808. By now, the United States had doubled its size by buying the territory of Louisiana from France, and more planters wanted slaves to grow cotton and sugar there. Thus, some Africans, Europeans, and Americans risked fines, imprisonment, and even death to continue trading slaves.

Leading abolitionists in England included Sharp, Macaulay, Wilberforce, Buxton, and Clarkson.

41

British Patrol Africa's Waters

British patrol boats sailed up and down the West Coast of Africa, stopping any ships they suspected of carrying slaves. It wasn't easy to catch these ships. Shipbuilders made faster ships that the traders now used, and some slavers tossed the slaves overboard when the patrols approached. One English captain in the illegal slave trade commanded a ship called the *Brilliante*. When four British cruisers approached, the captain ordered his crew to tie the slaves to the anchor chain and

The British ships capture a slave ship.

drop the anchor into the sea. They all drowned.

In spite of these difficulties, British ships captured 1,635 slave ships, and freed more than 160,000 people. Some were taken to Freetown—a city that the British had founded for freed slaves in 1787. (It is now the capital of the African country of Sierra Leone.) Other slaves were taken to Liberia, an African country founded by the United States in 1816. Some free blacks from the United States also settled in Liberia.

Heavy iron cuffs were used to shackle slaves.

Now that British ships were patrolling the West Coast of Africa, many slaving ships took the long trip around Cape Hope on the southern tip of the continent, looking for safer waters. By now, many Arabs from the Middle East had set up trading posts on Africa's East Coast. With the cooperation of Swahili slave traders, Arabs traded for slaves in Africa's interior. Thousands of slaves

A Famous African Slaver

Africans in the interior called one slaver *Tipoo Tib*, meaning "the sound of guns," because that's what they heard when he raided their villages. Tipoo Tib and other Arab traders forced black slaves to serve in several ways. The traders often traded ivory along with trading slaves and, some men had to carry heavy elephant tusks on their long walk from the interior to the coast. Some slaves were forced to raid their own tribes to get more slaves. Girls and women often became household servants or were forced to become Arabs' wives.

were fastened together in coffles and forced to march hundreds of miles to the coast. From there they were taken by boat to Zanzibar, an island 24 miles (39 km) off the coast. (Zanzibar is now part of Tanzania.)

The East Coast Slaving Capital

In 1832, Zanzibar's largest town, also called Zanzibar, became the capital of a large Arab state as well as the East Coast's chief slave market. Each year, twenty thousand to forty thousand slaves were brought to Zanzibar, and buyers from up and

down the coast crowded into the market square whenever a new shipload of slaves arrived. One-third of them were sold to Zanzibar planters to grow cloves, cacao, and coconut palms. Coconut oil was used to make soap. The oil was also spread on male slaves' bodies to make them shine before they went on sale at the market.

Young boys and girls brought the highest prices, and old people brought the lowest. Sometimes, as many as 150 people were packed into a cage and sold by the cageful. Slaves who

Markets still thrive in Africa today.

Arabs took thousands of slaves to the island of Zanzibar every year.

hadn't been sold were kept in damp, dark Zanzibar caves until they could be shipped to Arabia, Iraq, Persia (now Iran), or Turkey, where they brought ten times more money than Arab traders had paid for them.

American slavers also found their way to Zanzibar. American ships, many of them from Salem, Massachusetts, clogged its harbor. At the Zanzibar slave market, their crews exchanged cheap cotton fabric for slaves and ivory. British patrol ships guarding the harbor could do little about it. American sea captains avoided arrest by flying foreign flags and registering their ships under false names and numbers.

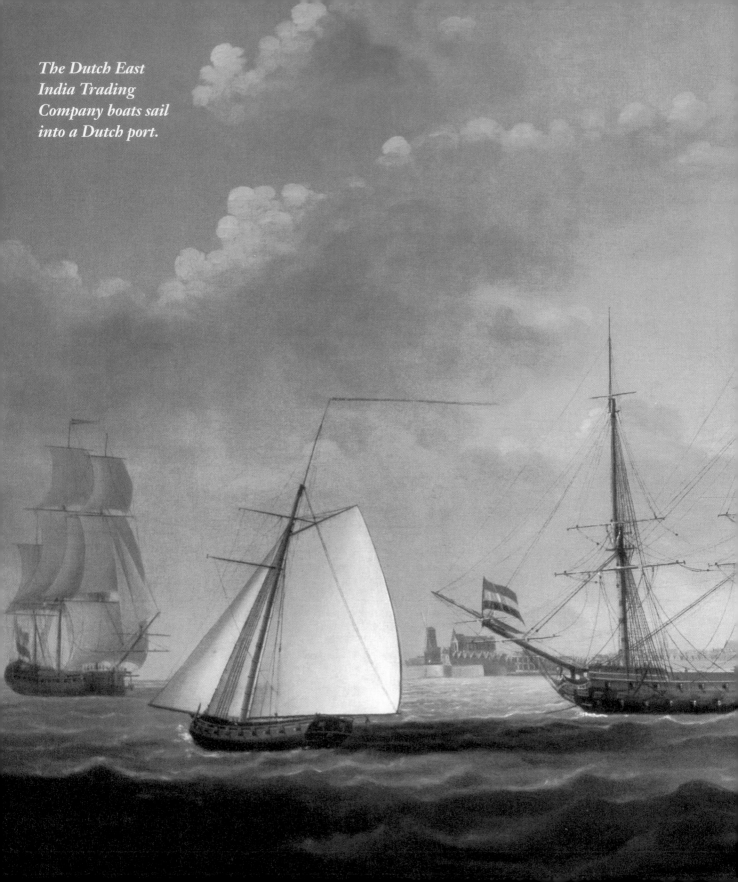

The Dutch East India Trading Company boats sail into a Dutch port.

Chapter Five

Europeans in South Africa

The first white people to settle at the southernmost tip of Africa worked for the Dutch East India Company. They arrived in 1632 to set up a base where the Dutch ships could get fresh vegetables and meat for their crews. Most black people left the area when the whites arrived, so slaves were brought from other parts of Africa to work on the company's farms.

Later, some of the Dutch East India Company's employees started their own

This 1804 painting shows a slave in South Africa returning from a hunt with his Boer master.

farms and became known as **Boers**, a Dutch word meaning "farmers." Soon German and French farmers joined them. As a group, they began calling themselves "Afrikaners," and a new language, Afrikaans, evolved. By 1700, whites had taken over most of the fertile farmland in the area. The blacks who still lived there became their servants or their slaves.

The Dutch and the British fought over South Africa for many years. By 1814, the British ruled, and in 1834, they abolished slavery. With their slaves freed, several thousand Afrikaners gave up their farms, loaded their belongings into

The Dutch East India Company

Competition for trading was fierce among many countries, and the Dutch government gave the Dutch East India Company special rights to help protect and increase its trade business. With the government's permission, the Dutch East India Company could trade, make treaties with local officials, build forts, and keep an army. The company's headquarters were in the Dutch East Indies (now Indonesia). Its ships traveled back and forth from the East Indies to Europe, stopping for supplies at their base at the tip of South Africa (now called the Cape of Good Hope).

ox-drawn wagons, and headed into the interior. Fighting off Bantu-speaking people who tried to stop them, the Afrikaners settled inland.

Dr. David Livingstone, a Scottish missionary in Africa described what happened when Afrikaners came to a village. "According to their custom, they demanded twenty or thirty [native] women to weed their gardens. I saw these women [leaving their villages] . . . carrying food on their heads, children on their backs, and hoes on their shoulders."

David Livingstone planned to encourage Africans to become Christians and to develop legal businesses to take the place of the slave trade. One evening when Livingstone and some other missionaries were resting outside their tents, a group of slaves approached. They were fastened to each other by heavy wooden yokes and guarded by Africans. The white men knew that if they interfered, the Portuguese slave traders in the area might attack them or destroy their supplies. "How can we not?" Livingstone asked. The white men stood up and

David Livingstone, a Scottish missionary, tried to stop the African slave trade.

the slavers ran into the forest. The missionaries freed eighty-four men, women, and children.

David Livingstone died in Africa. He was not able to stop the slave trade. When his notes returned to Europe, several other European missionaries, as well as explorers, also came to Africa. Some of the books they wrote gave Europeans the impression that slavery was natural to Africans. They even suggested that Africans could not take care of themselves and needed whites to take care of them.

How the Trade Affected Africa

The slave trade broke up families and whole communities. **Demographers**—scientists who study population sizes and distribution—say it's impossible to figure out how many more people would live in Africa today if there had been no slave trade. They also cannot determine how the land would have been changed if there had been no slave trade. Would some areas be more agricultural? Would others be more industrial? What would Africa be like now if there had been no slave trade or if Europeans had not expanded it? No one knows the answers to these questions. Only one thing is certain: Africa lost millions of its young men, women, and children to slavery.

Timeline

1433	European sea captains begin to explore coast of West Africa.
1442	A Portuguese sea captain returns to Portugal with twelve slaves.
1492	Columbus discovers the New World.
1501	Spain takes first Africans to its Caribbean colonies (West Indies).
1619	Twenty Africans are brought to Jamestown, Virginia, the first English settlement in North America.
1772	All slaves in Britain are freed.
1807	Slave trade is abolished in Britain.
1808	Slave trade is abolished in the United States.
1861–1865	The American Civil War ends Atlantic slave trade and slavery in the United States is abolished.
1888	Brazil frees its slaves.

Glossary

agent—a person who does business for others

barracoon—a pen or jail where slaves or convicts were kept

Boer—a Dutch word meaning farmer

cameo—a small sculpture

cargo—the products carried on ships

coffle—a line of slaves attached to each other by chains, metal rings, or heavy wooden yokes

cowrie shell—the shell of a sea snail; once used as money on the West Coast of Africa

custom house—a building where shipping records are kept

demographer—a scientist who studies population sizes and distributions

glutted—overloaded

hold—space under a ship's decks used to store cargo

helmsman—the person who steers a ship

indentured servants—people who worked for several years without pay

indigo—a plant used to dye fabric blue

longboat—the largest rowboat on a sailing vessel, used as a lifeboat or lowered into the sea to take members of the crew to other ships

moat—a trench filled with water that encircles a castle or fort

ophthalmia—an inflammation, or swelling, of the eye that sometimes caused blindness

pest house—a place where sick people were kept

plantation—a large farming estate cultivated by people who live on them

refuse—trash

To Find Out More

Books

Barboza, Steven. *Legend of Gorée Island*. New York: Dutton, 1994.

Black, Wallace. *Slaves to Soldiers, African American Fighting Men in the Civil War*. New York: Franklin Watts, 1998.

Cameron, Ann (Adapter), *The Kidnapped Prince, the Life of Olaudah Equiano*. New York: Alfred Knopf, 1995.

Lester, Julius. *From Slave Ship to Freedom Road*. New York: Dial, 1998.

Myers, Walter Dean. *Amistad*. New York: Dutton, 1997.

Newman, Shirlee P. *Slavery in the United States*. Danbury, CT: Franklin Watts, 2000.

———. *Child Slavery in Modern Times*. Danbury, CT: Franklin Watts, 2000.

Ofosu-Appiah, L.H. *People in Bondage, African Slavery since the 15th Century*. Minneapolis, MN: Runestone Press, 1993.

Sullivan, George. *Slave Ship, the Story of the Henrietta Marie*. New York: Dutton, 1994.

Organizations and Online Sites

African American Cultural Alliance
P.O. Box 22173
Nashville, TN 37202
A group that promotes African culture through educational programs and the performing arts.

African Art Museum of Maryland
5430 Vantage Point Road
Columbia, MD 21044
This museum displays art and cultural objects of Africa.

The DuSable Museum of African-American History
740 East 56th Place
Chicago, IL 60637-1495
http://www.dusablemuseum.org/
A museum devoted to African and African-American subjects.

Homowo Foundation for African Arts and Culture
2915 NE 15th Avenue
Portland, OR 97202
This organization promotes African culture through the performing arts.

The Charles H. Wright Museum
of African American History
315 East Warren Avenue at Bush Street
Detroit, MI 48201
http://www.maah-detroit.org/
This museum presents exhibits on African and African-American history and culture.

A Note on Sources

Most of my research has been done using good, old reliable books. Internet sources on the slave trade in Africa were not suitable, but adult books about Africa —some new, some old— were valuable, taken home from the library by the dozen, and compared. *Silent Terror*, a *Journey through Contemporary Slavery* was given to me by the president of the Anti-Slavery Society in Boston, Massachusetts. It is mostly about slavery today, but discusses the past too. I also consulted books about individual African countries, a biography of David Livingstone, and several encyclopedias. Milton Meltzer's books for children and young adults are great. I am indebted to him. I made special trips to Charleston, South Carolina; Savannah, Georgia; Newport, Rhode Island; and several islands in the West Indies for background material for this book. I also explored the replica of the 1700s ship *Bark Endeavor*. After I completed my research and wrote the first draft, Dr. Michelle H. Martin, Assistant Professor, Children's and Young Adult Literature Specialist at the Stephen F. Austin State University, reviewed the manuscript and offered helpful suggestions on how to improve the book. Thanks to Paula and Mark for the trip to Charleston, Jeff, Jan, and Jack for trips to the Caribbean, and Deb for technical assistance.

—*Shirlee P. Newman*

Index

Numbers in *italics* indicate illustrations.

About the Author

Shirlee Petkin Newman has written twenty books for children, including *The Incas*, *The Inuits*, *The Creek*, and *The Pequots, Slavery in the United States*, and *Child Slavery in Modern Times*. Her books include biographies, a picture book, fiction, and folk tales. She has been an associate editor at *Child Life Magazine* and taught writing for chidren at Brandeis University. She has traveled to North Africa, the Middle East, Europe, the Caribbean (West Indies), Central and South America, and Mexico. She has been interested in the subject of slavery almost all of her life, and has also written a historical fiction story set in Boston in abolitionist times.